MW00877093

TIME SPENT FALLING

by

Nick Holmes

Edited by Angela Gygi

Copyright © 2016 Nick Holmes

All rights reserved.

ISBN-10: 1535188308
ISBN-13: 978-1535188302

Cover model: Elizabeth Porter
fonts: www.kingthingsfonts.co.uk

A NOTE

I don't suppose I ever thought I'd
write a book of poetry. Somehow it
feels like a sensible accident that
happened as my life was changing near
the end of my twenties. This collection
was written during a fantastical series
of lonely nights and romantic escapes.
Over the period of a few years there
were suddenly hundreds of pages - some
scribbled on hotel stationary, emails
to myself, notes made between
destructive evening breaths and
glorious morning carnality - but I only
offer a few of them here. Consume them
as you wish. The narrative of each
chapter will not isolate you from
skipping about (my preferred method).
My hopeful wish is that any one of
these, with luck perhaps a few, will
serve you as they served me. A memory
recalled, a flavor not forgotten, a
lover called to attention, or the
simple escape inside yourself.

FOR ARUNA,

YOU ARE ENTRANCING.

A PLEASURE TO KNOW YOU.

My sincere appreciation,

Nick

For Peach.

PLACES

MEXICO

~
Hold still
and let my eyes
dance the breath out of you.
Don't move
I'll push the world away
so we'll have room;
for love,
Let the gate swing open
let the hinges wail
in celebration
of the light's arrival
to take care of us.
~

~
I'm forged from the country earth
and endless skies.
The warrior in me loves the city
the business, the people.
The rest of me belongs to the country
where I know I can hold still.
~

~

My personal Elysium
I guarded you so carefully
against the fragile culture
of a life lived amongst
the misunderstood
    who are the first
        themselves
to misunderstand.
The room I built for us
had no door,
only a high window
for sunshine to come in
during the perfect parts of our day.
I want the walls down
for the clouds and the moon
to pass by us
as everyone else.
The self-inflicted notion
of sadness
guilt
takes me from the
unbent time we spend
making love into simple shapes.
I dwell in the heavy air
and crowd my chest with
a thousand wishes for things
to unfold
into a now
I can recognize.
. . .

```
. . .
Then
almost at once
the warm comes in
as I speak softly to myself
of the mighty truth
that I am not as I think
this moment;
there is no shadowed box
we must live in,
no solace needed
for sadness carried
on the fallen leaves
of the autumn hours
I spend without you.
The audacity
to think myself melancholy
when, in clarity of fact,
I am
  most magnificently
In love.
~
```

~
Touch me,
anywhere.
Don't run
unless it's looking back
along the sand
rippling and polished
by the liquid diamond sea
Waiting for me
to catch you
and I will.
~

~
If Picasso wrote a piano song
and Beethoven bent a brush
the distance between art
  and archetype
would blacken
into a star filled fantasy
constellations keep for themselves
away from the myth
but full of the magic I feel
in the bend of your lily stem back.
~

~
That's our ocean.
Always growling
in motion
twisted by the moon,
waiting
with thundering impatience
to wrap around our ankles
like shackles made of slow kisses
that we might be taken
the most willing prisoners.
~

NEW ORLEANS

~
In my dream for the day
I'm just around your next corner
climbing up the hill to you.
I haven't slept.
Not really.
I get by
with restless naps
alongside a memory
of you
giving me your weight
and your perfect little noises
and purrs.
I can feel the world
swirling around me
newly mine.
Taking stock of all of me
there is a part
that is yours
filled with pink pearls and poetry.
Warm desert air and long
perfect looks.
Wrapped in each other
even without touching.
~

~
The trees sway as we would.
Lasting long into the morning
to drink the early rain
and stretch toward the sun.
A view of the clouds
only lovers have.
~

~
Trying to make the most
from slow empty days.
It's the noise I miss
not the easy company.
Remembering
to pick up my pen
and little else
I try to serve some good
I don't completely understand.
What I have made of my life
is irrelevant
to what I will make of it now.
In so much quiet
I realize
many of the comforts of love
are the sounds your mind makes
when you know
someone else is there.
~

~
I can feel this day...
Where I held you last night
aloft and drenched
in attention from my hands
and mouth
the muscles used for
pulling
  pushing
wail from their satisfactions
with a well-worn tremble.

The monster of this lonely evening
springs from my singular shadow
to hold my eyes open
and lift away my throat
as I make half a home
under this blanket.

I tie ribbons on the trees
marking a path of memories
to make daydream distractions
in the lesser moments
between the second I saw you last
and a tomorrow
that starts with your smile.
~

~

If there were some bit of faith
or congregation
made to fill the empty moments
  of this night
with the blood and bread
  of your lips,
that kept the cold moon light
like an empty pew
off my shoulders,
then I would submit
weary for your gospel
a servant
by my brow
and strong hands
to the choirs of your thighs
and the commandments
you write with indelicate want
on my tablet back.

~

SAN FRANCISCO

~
I'll make pyramids
from the sand
of San Francisco,
the sphinx from your table napkin,
chorus dancers of nearby strangers
anything
to make you look at me
again.
The marble of your glance
veins of green and blue
have made a slave of me.
A wretch
dedicated to the feel of your cloth
and the simple gestures
your hands make.
Command tasks of me
push me to the floor
in corruption.
Ease yourself onto me
and set about the work
of a master.
Beckon more of me
with parts of you that
can only command
with sweat and vibrations.
As ordered
I'll serve you
platters of myself
finger fed
to your blood red lips
with unrelenting carefulness.
. . .

...
I will seek
only to pleasure you
like it is the task
of my life.

Churn your cream white cloak
into my rich indulgence.

Take me in
as your servant
and I will
humbly destroy
Every. Single. Thing.
that tortures you.
~

~
Move like you always do
task for task
about the world
and you'll be dancing for me.
Speak as you would
a shapely chorus
the lyrics of your life
and it will be a song for me.
~

~

Sun topped trees bow in the breeze
like thoughtful gentlemen,
Crisscrossing power lines
  censor the view
    of hill nested patios,
A king palm
that predates any notion I have
  of love
shifts it's weight
in a gust that tussles the fronds;
Reminds me of your beach walk hair
  puts a strong feeling
    of weakness
      in my knees
I'm grateful to endure
at every onslaught memory of you.
You'll be here soon;
thief of my breath,
and I will stand
with all of my might
to hold you.

~

~

A wind born from want
draws the sky apart
rushes down empty avenues
to whistle at my window
carrying the rumble of a train
too far away to ride a sunshine breeze
rattles this half sleep
I tip my eyes
toward an empty pillow
wishing you were my gentle freight
on our way to the next anywhere.

~

~

What has been made of August
this summer
unlike any other in my life
is a kind of peace
I imagine soldiers
who have slept under war's weather
only truly know;
a knowing taste of quiet
having seen the noise.
My widened shoulders
no longer feeling the weight
of a floundering infancy
spent scowling so intently
to ward off whatever foes
I made for myself.
Trenches leading into the mist
of a headlong unknown
wake me now and then:
when the damp walls
and exposed roots give way
to bury me in restlessness.
Assuaged by the lulling purr
of the afternoon breeze
across a hilltop
raised a million Sundays ago
just for us to see the sunset.
. . .

. . .
Such a gift to spend this charge
toward the autumn
with you at my morning fingertips
discovering new pinks
serenaded by our sky colored lake
and tiny night creatures
curious about our noises.
I taste you every time my eyes close
awake
in this delicious dream
of us.
~

~

They haven't made stars
that guide
or constellations
worth believing in
that would make the path
to us
quick to find
or simple to follow.
It's a different flavor of rain
that falls on lovers
drops full of afternoon wine
and under table touches
make glistening trips
to restless tongues.
We'll trade breaths
and fill our lungs
with baited screams
of 'I love you'.

~

~

There must be a moon
or two
missing from some system
of unnamed stars
a tipped over chair
in a quickly abandoned universe,
left to whatever night
can be made
from scraped together shade.
Here instead
is the tide pulling glow
of celestial majesty
blinking back at me
through eyelashed eclipses
casting wave tip glints
along your shoreline lips,
stirring spirits of quake
and lust
in gods
who only come out to dance
at twilight.

~

~

Hundreds of unplanned miles from here
I sat still
very still
for the first in a long string
of ever after intentions
and wept.
Tears pushed into the dry world
by laughter
made with my whole chest.
In a blurred wetness
usually saved for newborns
and their proud fathers.
I cried
for me
and the triumph of my own happiness.
How then
do I stop now?
For what reason?
My kindness is gone from you
not that I am unkind.
My will is not directed to you
but I am not without will.
I am all I am;
some with your help,
and I will never be else.
Just as you'd wish
if we had survived.

~

~

My mind is awash
in thoughts of you
swimming and weightless
in a four post sea.
My mouth wet
wanting the landscape of your stomach
to look across.

~

THE DESERT

~

The winter is coming
with unforgiving certainty.
I can tell.
I've seen the cold before
in a different lifetime
lived only years ago.
All the signs of the fall
point to it's arrival
to make dust
of fire red leaves.
The creatures feel it too
and with unconscious wisdom
prepare.
The geese pause
at a nearby river
to gather themselves
then depart as soon
making their bag-pipe music
a war song against the season.
Driven
not away
but forward
by a self
they unquestioningly understand.
The winter is coming
to claim everything
but not me.

~

~

You are a wonder;
the curtsy of blond on my hips
  a new addiction,
the floor-less dances through tables
around barely breathing statues,
well earned bids of good morning
across scandalized pillows,
winks that seem in slow motion,
the shudder of your ribs
under my traversing hands
  makes me feel beautiful,
the glorious days
spent in your blankets
creating the weather,
and the only real sleep
I know anymore
 new worlds quieted by their goddess.

~

~

Through this mist
of a made-up
late summer London
I watched you
like a spy
tilted hat
and hidden intentions
to consume your body
in the name of a republic
I wait needingly
for you to name
and call out.

~

~

If we were train robbers
chasing steel
of a hundred years ago
I'd swing your hand
with the vigor of a waltz
walking through the quieter
days.
Happy to be the one
to calm the devil in you
With the devil in me.

~

~

I was afraid
just as I woke
before my eyes
ever let in the light
that it was all a dream.
An apparition
ghosting through me
collecting my words
and praising me
just so.
Could my mind
betray me into believing
that these hands never
held you in place
while this Goddess
who could put words in the sky
answered my kisses?
If so,
keep me
alive in this storybook
and close quickly the cover.
Whatever dream this is
I want it.

~

~

The luxury
of any loneliness
left in my life
is that it reminds me
of you.

~

HAVANA

~
I burn slowly down
Your candle wick tongue
savoring the slide
from the unreasonable normal
to the brisk edge
of quivering insanity.
My just tensed brow
beaded with anticipation
for your dewy
soft touch
taking me in
with reckless devotion
to the eruption.
Our hips argue over
  under
    about.
Singe my fingers
and scorch my belly
with the blue flame
I light on your lips
and we'll make ashes
of this untouched day.
~

~

Hands pressed at my brow
to blot away the night
stamp the first morning view
of your elegantly mangled curves
and curls
into my mind's accruing memories;
joined with a thousand fantasies
the machine of this desire for you
has made.
When I'm lucky,
as this day clearly reveals I am,
you haven't stirred;
I grab your dream
by the shoulder blades
to fit your cheek
into the sling of my neck,
a trap I lay
that the moment you wake
turn to take stock
I can watch you look up at me.

~

~

And after the rain
then what?
After you've pulled the Tuesday fog
past my knees
and swallowed seasons
made of lingering leaf worry,
what shall I do
to repay such a favor?
Dole out the tolls and taxes
at your leisure.
I'll pay any penance
through your confession gates,
re-stretch your ferry ropes,
tip the demons who carry your bags;
squint my slanted martini warning
at the so-called heros
who shout at the rain.
Dance this falling ocean with me
and we'll remind
the sun starved flowers
why they grow.

~

~

Wishes made
on briefly falling stars
will bring us back
to this place.
To blood red wine
fire lit dances
and sand strewn blankets.
Our final night
made flesh
by last rights
given to a moth
made of paisley
and the waltz
from your pillow
to mine.

~

~

Swimming in an elixir ocean
we learned to pour our waves
a paradise away
from your PO box and bedsheets.
I swept every curse
wrongfully referred to as cares
under the marbled gray rug
of a rainy Los Angeles mountainside.
What must I give
or take
to remain here,
drawing my days in textures
  down pillow mornings
    cast iron afternoons;
losing the hours
in almond fire warmth
and drawers of iron daisies.
Flavors of juniper gin,
ideas about sunshine
sharpen along a twist of blond
that touches your lips
long enough to elicit my envy.
Open a book
or your dress;
I'll find some prose
that will make
this shadowless afternoon
into literature
leather-bound or otherwise.

~

PASADENA

~
Today aches.
Tonight will surely fail me.
I don't want any more sunshine
or thousand year old star winks;
only you.
~

~

Luck is not to do with it;
not at this point.
One hundred kisses ago
maybe I looked at my cards
calculated
counted blessings
in fingernail hash marks
on my shoulders.

The gift of my life
is not to do with figures and sums
making a science
out of the closing distance
between what I knew of my heart
and what I wondered
about yours.

North or south
along your map fold thighs,
west to your Andes,
east to the exotic tomorrow flavors
you can drum out of the wind.
I'm on board.
Saved by gold
whimsey labeled weekdays.
I was no less than a fool
to watch this close for so long
without seeing;
all the oceans belong to you.
(why else see them?)
Every mountain poised in tribute.
The stars and sand
there to sugar your sunsets.
. . .

...
Have it all
then let me have you;
I'll smooth the edges
these polished trophy days.
Watch closely
for the moon to smile at you
while I pull the stars down
and get your hair in my
teeth.
~

~

I always disagree
with the way every new year begins;
　　a dismantling of the holiday.
The wooded shelter
　for gifts and memories
sprung from some popup forest,
　　the effigies of new hope
　　　　dancing like gypsies
　　in the windows
　　of every home I pass,
Now put out to wilt
in the same daylight
that used to nurture them.
Strings of starlight
　　some wind tangled and expired
boxed away for an afternoon
of future frustration.
While the children
　　like watchful foreman
judge your abilities on a ladder.
Whatever God can be found in all this,
　　I thank him
　　　　for You
　　　　　　and your warm eyes
on the cold days of another December.
I've no use for spring anymore;
too fond of leather jackets
and any need you might have
to hold me a bit closer in the night.
~

~

I thought a walk
through the street lamps
or to the cinema
    anywhere
away from this exhausted ash tray
a still sulking pillow
might shorten the hours
till we're together.
Instead,
in a shirt that smells like you,
poured the wine
and laughed
because you give me too much beauty
not to smile.

~

~

Step into me
I'll hold you up
above the notions of decency
made for day creatures
and snow white liars.
We'll make an easy sport
out of acceptance
and walk the park
hands held or
dug into borrowed back pockets
no less entitled
to the sunshine
than the pairs who whisper
  often bark
across gold rings.

~

~

I have watched you
a long time now;
and my fingers have ached
to trace the sun's freckled footsteps
across your cheek
  down your back.
Years of stolen looks
masked with garish smirks
meant all the while
to stir your ideas
about how my hands might feel
  or how hard I kiss in the morning.
Imagining often
  past the barriers of an old life
of your fire red hair
collapsing my shoulders -
what pinks we might discover
if we gave each other patience,
    I have watched you.
Wanting you to know
the feeling of being longed for
with such fervent thirst
  to draw vitality
    from your perspiration
and to hold your hips aloft
  Sunday after Sunday
until God
made a new kind of sense for you.
I've made friends with the night
  conspired with Orion
to bend your Galway eyes
  to settle into mine
and let my open mouth
  take your needs away.

~

ROME

~
The shame
a statue must feel
at the sight
of your moonlit legs.
~

~
Life enunciates itself
in a place like Rome.
Every street has a moonlit story
regardless the sunlight.
What debt I owe
to hold your hand in this place.
I hope the night is everything
your mind practiced
without me.
~

~

Visited by a hungry winter
long left behind
I made a penny wish
in some leftover rain
for dreams of her
  feared forgotten.
The shopping bag people
  well practiced lovers
meander the sidewalks
I don't want their attention
  church smiles
they don't know what I know.
Too many cautions thrown
at curious eyes
  unpredictable evenings
any idea of adventure
  an unfamiliar dog
    a wet bench.
A tree's slow vengeance
against the pavement
gives me the grim idea that everything
is in pieces
even if it's not broken.
So I take my midnight walks
  chest empty
    eyes searching
all of me; incomplete
  incongruous.
There is no escaping this want
for your wine and ache flavored mouth
screaming to my rescue
against the distance.

~

~

Forgetfulness has a sweet
smokey taste.
I have groaned along highways
chopped trees to remnants
with all my swarthy infliction.
Plain as the surrender flag
I have given
  so I could take
and slept under the blankets of art.
What is the challenge?
Why win?
Only to last?
Stand on the pillar
with those who have lasted before
who helped
with their brows and vocal systems
to drive a love and longing
for a poem
you'd be lucky to help write
  likely never finish.
. . .

. . .
Bare your bosom
  protect your heart
    with acts of calculated indecency;
surprise yourself
with willingness to go along
through stretches and stretches
of September
  and
    perhaps
if your lips sing some silent
indescribable song
in the oaken cathedral moment -
you'll be invited to the prayer.
No less than a sacrifice
of blood and sex and kindness,
To connect inside the
dot-to-dot spectacle of success.
To breathe life
into such a reluctant creature
for hope
  of light
    and gold
and some reasonable idea
of why it was worth
everything you lost
to say you won.

~

~

The dancing parade we've made
along the cobbled streets
through pillar shadowed archways
is full of twisting steps skyward
and cape breeze kisses.
I would sing this place to you
if we hadn't learned the words
together.
The ocean sounds;
bees in December
winging their way
to a drizzled morning breakfast
. . .

...
I'll take of your mouth
and assorted S-curves.
My body's allegiance
to the new world
under your coat.
~

MALIBU

~

It's not that the sea
calls to me;
my former lives
spent elsewhere,
amidst the rocks and the trees
made my heart vibrate,
but my ears are pleased
by the water's music
and my lungs relax
in the salt sweet air.
There are rhythms of life
only audible
in moments and places
where you can see the earth bend.
I wasn't made
to stand on a sandy shoreline
or cut quickly healing paths
through the water.
Yet I belong here;
my arrival
always a return.

~

~
The stillness
along with the night quiet
screams over my dizzy thoughts
as I wait for sleep.
My eyes searched for you
in today's lone venture into sunlight.
Come and find me love
before the dark wins you back
for yet another day
away from me.
~

~

There is no high court
or bench sitting wise man
that upon seeing
your pink tongue
moisten those red lips
could find fault
in all the crimes
I'd commit
to take your body
and breath.

~

~

My foggy morning mind
is eased by this
rare moment of proximity
you are streets
  not states
    away.
It won't be enough
until I'm breathing your hair
wrapped with your sleep-strength arms
  my slow descent
on your beautiful protrusions.
Thoroughly winging on this
daily dream of you
I step across sunlight constellations
yesterday's denim and your picture.
I set my eyes
past the empty breath afternoon
through a window you opened;
we kiss a thousand times over coffee
  and I lose my place in a book
    dripping honey down your back.
This is how the dancing starts.

~

~

In all the blue of night
my eyes relax
  over whatever beauty
    the moon draws edges around.
I search
my room
 the backs of my hands
for a trace of you.
Plying the walls
with warm candlelight
  and music
    I hope will stir them to grow
into imagined castles
  where I can wait
    for the next dream of you
      to arrive like the dawn
    and polish to gold
this navy evening.

~

~

Somewhere between Saturday's sins
and Sunday's religion
we caught each other
staring back
  wanting quietly
wishing for warmth
more than a new breath
or a new sunrise.
In a wisdom beyond our judgment
the stars arrived
forcing the skies to readiness
and you leapt into my eyes
  melted in my hands
divinely prescribed
by the otherworldly will
of completeness.
There we were
replete with the other
arrested and rushed
through echoing seconds
full with want
that we could have time.

~

~
Leaning in a sun filled corner
listening to the day wake up.
Pieces of me taking turns
humming your name.
~

KANSAS

~

The apartment is a still life
of this morning
when our lives were different
before anything was said.
When you still loved me
and thought I was kind.

~

~

I look everywhere
inside myself
to find answers for you.
Now my eyes are tired and
I'm still wandering
searching
for a way back.

I'm hiding from you
in plain sight
only pretending you don't see me.
I remember a time
when only I could see you
my bright shining future.
You didn't know me then
as you would.
It took just the right amount
of time
and handwriting
to make you a part of me.
Delighted to learn your magic
and to teach you mine
We spent Christmas on this street
and made a family
alone together.

~

~

I knew what it was
to love you
a thousand years ago
between the playgrounds
and the sidewalks.

We were young,
took our chances
counted hope as courage.

You arrived from the wheat fields
and the clouds
pouring your wine
long left to breath
a shared glass
   full at any measure
vinegar notes
the untamed spice
of a sleepless night.

Dancing against ourselves
after the lust red years
we filled the air with sighs
made eye to eye.

Were we more clever as children
when we laughed and looked away
Before it hurt to pretend so briefly.

~

~

In the granite light
of a Saturday afternoon
I poured a chair for you
and waited.
A double
made triple
twice in a row
found curves
in straight and narrow thoughts.
Neat bourbon giving soft edges
to the memory of this morning
without you.
My mind wanders
to the length and breadth
of the trees
who gave their lives
to the amber hue flavor
of today's forgetful practice.
I've made a view I like
across the ice
through the flowers
imitating their own beauty.
Courteous questions
answered courteously
"I'm fine"
Where are you?

~

~

Dust stings my eyes
turns my face to find the sun;
the sound of a messenger wind
carrying the ocean's romance
stretched thin by lonely plains
hollowed by cold mountains
fills my ears with it's desperation.
I smile with low shoulders
and wink at a tomorrow
only we know,
the air falls still
and I see your face.
Stepping through today
forward
on my way back to you.

~

~

Where will we go
from this place?
Back the way we came
I suppose;
once more
upon the edge
of an ending
we made so carefully
for each other.

~

ROOM 48

~
What is this
castle of ours?
A haven from the world;
an escape into each other.
So much
of what I need
fills the walls
and fogs the windows
in any place you have been.
A memory music box
that unwraps me
a souvenir from a place
I always wanted to go.
I feel you
in every fourth floor inch
of this castle
made of us.
~

~

Walking in the rain
I wish to hear your breath
instead of the slosh
of a near empty flask.
Thinking of a girl
who knows
what not to say
holds my hand
shares her cigarette.

The street lamps
add gold to the sidewalk
and make shadows of the huddling
trees.
I walk this street often
but it's quieter now.
Understanding that cowboys wear boots
to hear themselves move on.

The old houses are perfectly lit
and still.
Sheltering people with no reason
to be out in this wet world.
As I would be
were your head in my lap.

There are not even any cats
to be suspicious of me
as I move at half speed
through the mist.
. . .

...
The rain pauses
and the drain whispers like a brook.
Leaves
under my feet
not yet cleared away
by the gardeners
who erase the autumn.

The sound of the storm
preserved by the large trees;
each branch's bounty
of leftover drops.

A wilted refrigerator box
that was yesterdays fortress
or castle
to a young hero
the game abandoned.

I search the glow around every light
for a glimpse of your cheek.
The yellow gray sky
of a well lit metropolis
reminds me
I'm alone
in a now hidden crowd.
~

~

The night has arrived
on time
to free me
from another empty afternoon.
Void
without you here.
I have my menials
to occupy me
but they're of little help.
My hands are clumsy
performing tasks
that don't unbutton you.
My mind too busy
painting pictures
of your mouth
on mine;
dreaming up
cafes in Paris
and dance floors
in Manhattan.
Anywhere
I can twirl you.

~

~

There are beautiful things
to say
and feel
about all the ways you are.
Prose aside
in this moment
all I want
is to make you
feel my weight and
taste my sweat
until you know
the parts of you
that belong to me.

~

~

A threshold away
from the terry cloth forest
we've explored with knees and hands,
I sit
in the opaque afternoon
watching you through fogged glass
    drenched,
        gleaming,
            and beautiful.
You like me there
amidst whatever silliness.

~

~

The days suit me best
as intermediaries
between unexecuted rendezvous
and the poised victory lap
I take
wine in hand
around whatever side of the bed
the chaos of our collision
has declared yours.
A knight
or Steve McQueen
crowned in the victory
of losing myself to you.

~

~

My world
is a twilight dance
in zero gravity;
Woven together by mystics
a waltz without steps
to the time and timber
of your tongues orchestration
Red and floating
in a tipped over chalice
Drank down by half
Before your pulse
Becomes the rhythm
I pillage you by.

~

~

It's nothing of effort
to picture you
in places
we've never been.
Your face
filling up unfamiliar skies
your lines framed
in new doorways.
It's less to recall
the fit of your hips
against mine;
eyelashes on my cheek
as your mouth makes
a vibrant wake
that crests
into the corners of me
who cannot forget you.

~

NEW YORK

~

This anniversary of myself
began with a simple restlessness
that I waited
worked for
my whole life.

~

~

The sleeping cats and calm pigeons
of Morton Avenue
taught me stillness
on my torrent
to meet you for lunch.
I bought you a rose along the way,
filled it with hopes of forgiveness
for the moments
I touched you too soft
or kissed you too hard.
Then you rescued me from worry
with your angel eyes
and sinner smile.

~

~

My body woke for a mission
a charge upon pink borders
ordered by your espionage lips.
Instead
this morning's battle
sets me against
empty arms.
I rage at the ache
Petitioner of your tongue
on a blind crusade
across warm fields,
to our war-painted victory.

~

~

The sum of however many miles
I travel from there to here;
to you
to paradise
is less than any man
in any time
has ventured
to rescue his soul
on knees bent
for prayers of perversion.
A taste of heaven
with your hands in my hair
and the tension of your thighs
to muffle the righteousness.

~

~

Be unreasonable, be beautiful
as though you could help it,
    be silent,
        be restless or nonsensical,
    be violent,
be pink or pinstriped,
    unpredictable without worry;
be here.
For god's sake
    just be here.

~

~

There is no planning
for dances
across borders
or the pull of a rug
walked over without the caution
of tradition.
The stretch of a snow colored pillow;
an ice hue blue
whispered warm with the words
of nearly a stranger.

Let my voice
burn your tongue
with every whiskey
and give my teeth
one thought in twenty
when your lovers hands
reach your stomach;
when the weight of a warm bath
pulls at your hair.
The sun takes it turn
for everyone;
I want the gold of you,
draped over a lovers intention,
to know the night's
not given to sleep
but to the endeavor
of a dance with starlight
strung along a tangled wish
for the morning
to arrive gently
and with company.

~

THANK YOU ROD

Nick Holmes is an actor, photographer, poet, and pretend cowboy residing in Los Angeles.

@narcissusholmes

www.nickholmesonline.com

58947173R00064

Made in the USA
Charleston, SC
23 July 2016